Contents

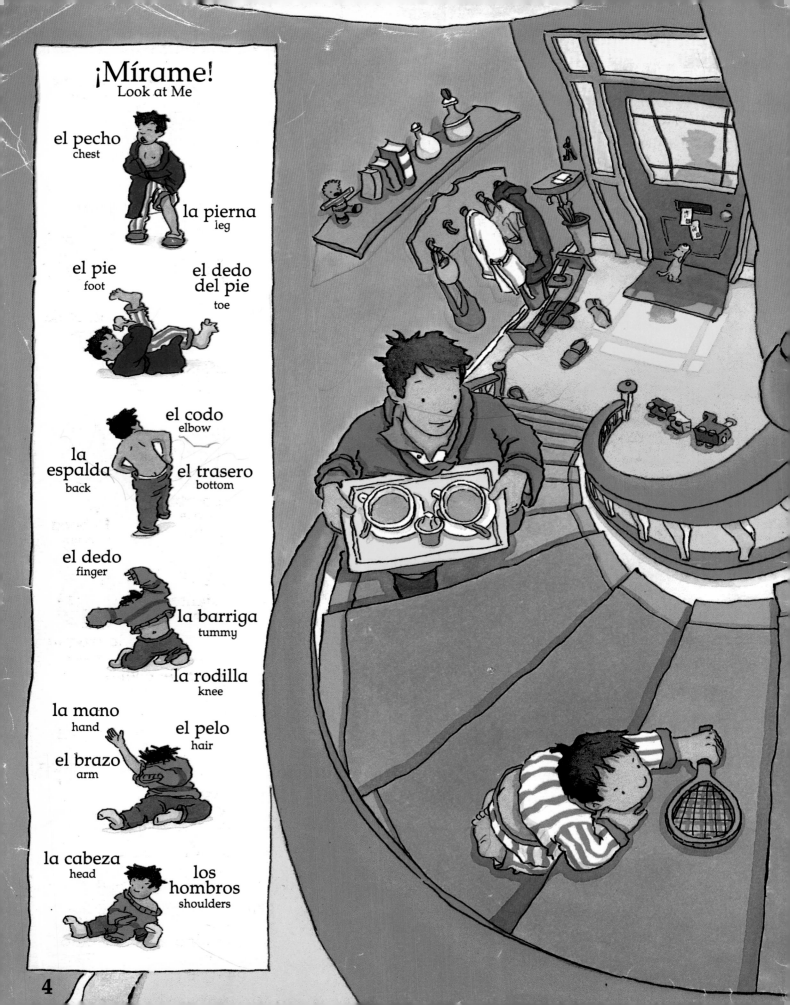

¡Mírame!
Look at Me

el pecho
chest

la pierna
leg

el pie
foot

el dedo
del pie
toe

el codo
elbow

la
espalda
back

el trasero
bottom

el dedo
finger

la barriga
tummy

la rodilla
knee

la mano
hand

el pelo
hair

el brazo
arm

la cabeza
head

los
hombros
shoulders

4

OXFORD

First

Spelling Words

Melling

Morris

OXFORD

UNIVERSITY PRESS

For Bosiljka, Branko and Igor Sunajko.

D.M.

OXFORD
UNIVERSITY PRESS

Great Clarendon Street, Oxford OX2 6DP

Oxford University Press is a department of the University of Oxford.
It furthers the University's objective of excellence in research, scholarship,
and education by publishing worldwide in

Oxford New York

Auckland Bangkok Buenos Aires Cape Town Chennai
Dar es Salaam Delhi Hong Kong Istanbul Karachi Kolkata
Kuala Lumpur Madrid Melbourne Mexico City Mumbai Nairobi
São Paulo Shanghai Taipei Tokyo Toronto

British Library Cataloguing in Publication Data available

ISBN 0–19–910953-2

Spanish translation by Ana Cristina Llompart

3 5 7 9 10 8 6 4

Printed in Italy by G. Canale & C. S.p.A.

la cara
face

la mejilla
cheek

la oreja
ear

el ojo
eye

la barbilla
chin

la boca
mouth

los dientes
teeth

la lengua
tongue

el cuello
neck

la nariz
nose

la niña
girl

el niño
boy

Nuestra casa
Our House

el tejado
roof

**el cubo
de la basura**
dustbin

la verja
gate

las escaleras
stairs

la chimenea
chimney

la valla
fence

el garaje
garage

la ventana
window

la puerta
door

el perro
dog

el gato
cat

el conejo
rabbit

la araña
spider

el caracol
snail

las cartas
letters

**la saca
de correos**
postbag

la hoja
leaf

la flor
flower

el árbol
tree

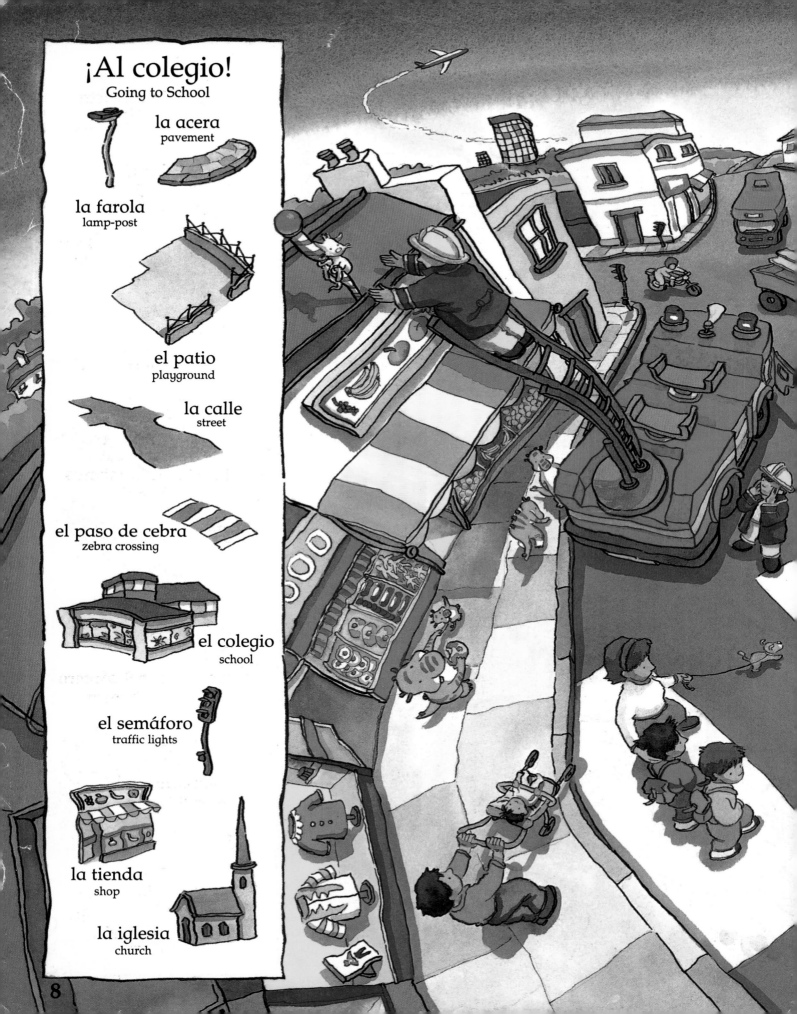

¡Al colegio!
Going to School

la acera
pavement

la farola
lamp-post

el patio
playground

la calle
street

el paso de cebra
zebra crossing

el colegio
school

el semáforo
traffic lights

la tienda
shop

la iglesia
church

8

la bicicleta
bicycle

el coche
car

el autobús
bus

la moto
motorbike

el coche de bomberos
fire engine

el camión
truck

el helicóptero
helicopter

la ambulancia
ambulance

el avión
plane

Nuestra clase
Our Classroom

la cartera
schoolbag

el libro
book

la tartera
lunch box

la pizarra
blackboard

la tiza
chalk

el globo
terráqueo
globe

el pupitre
desk

el imán
magnet

la papelera
bin

el casete
cassette recorder

la cinta de casete
cassette

la regla
ruler

el ordenador
computer

el mapa
map

el disquete
disk

el dado
dice

el teclado
keyboard

el ratón
mouse

11

La clase de arte
What Fun it is to Paint!

negro
black

azul
blue

marrón
brown

verde
green

gris
grey

naranja
orange

rosa
pink

morado
purple

rojo
red

blanco
white

amarillo
yellow

el delantal
overalls

el pegamento
glue

el dibujo
painting

el pincel
paintbrush

las pinturas
paints

el lápiz
pencil

el papel
paper

las tijeras
scissors

el rotulador
felt pen

el caballete
easel

13

Cuando sea mayor
When I Grow Up

el cartero
postman

el carpintero
carpenter

la médica
doctor

la mujer policía
police officer

la veterinaria
vet

el futbolista
footballer

el bombero
firfeighter

**el conductor
de autobuses**
bus driver

el conductor
de trenes
train driver

el cantante
de pop
pop star

el piloto
pilot

la bailarina
dancer

el submarinista
diver

el cocinero
cook

el astronauta
astronaut

el socorrista
lifeguard

15

Hace mucho tiempo
Long Ago

Los dinosaurios:
Dinosaurs

hace 200 millones de años
200 million years ago

Tiranosaurio
Tyrannosaurus Rex

Stegosaurus
Stegosaurus

Diplodocus
Diplodocus

Triceratops
Triceratops skeleton

el fósil
fossil

el hueso
bone

El hombre de la Edad de Piedra:
Stone Age Man

hace 10.000 años
10,000 years ago

la cueva
cave

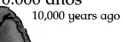

el pedernal
flint

la pintura rupestre
cave painting

el fuego
fire

El antiguo Egipto:
Ancient Egyptians

hace 5.000 años
5,000 years ago

la pirámide
pyramid

la esfinge
sphinx

el faraón
Pharaoh

El Imperio Romano:
Ancient Romans

hace 2.000 años
2,000 years ago

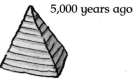

la cerámica
pottery

las monedas
coins

el soldado
soldier

17

De compras
Shopping

 **el carro**
trolley

 la cesta
basket

 **la caja registradora**
cash register

 la barra de pan
bread

 el bollo
bun

 la mermelada
jam

 **los cereales**
cereal

 las patatas
potatoes

 las salchichas
sausages

 los espaguetis
spaghetti

18

la leche
milk

el yogur
yoghurt

el queso
cheese

los huevos
eggs

la manzana
apple

el plátano
banana

la naranja
orange

el tomate
tomato

la zanahoria
carrot

la lechuga
lettuce

Una comida de monstruous

A Monster lunch

la cocina
cooker

la nevera
fridge

la lavadora
washing machine

la cacerola
saucepan

la plancha
iron

la taza
cup

el bol
bowl

el cuchillo
knife

el tenedor
fork

la hervidora
eléctrica
kettle

el plato
plate

20

la cuchara
spoon

el platito
saucer

la silla
chair

la tetera
teapot

el cojín
cushion

el sofá
sofa

el estéreo
stereo

la mesa
table

la televisión
television

el vídeo
video recorder

la aspiradora
vacuum cleaner

¡Vamos a jugar!
Let's Play

la casita de muñecas
doll's house

la muñeca
doll

el juego de mesa
game

el coche de carreras
racing car

el robot
robot

el rompecabezas
jigsaw puzzle

el osito de peluche
teddy

el tren de juguete
train set

el tambor
drum

la guitarra
guitar

el teclado
keyboard

el micrófono
microphone

la trompeta
trumpet

la flauta
recorder

los platillos
cymbals

los cascabeles
bells

la pandereta
tambourine

23

En la granja
At the Farm

el caballo
horse

la gallina
chicken

el gallo
cock

el pato
duck

el ganso
goose

la oveja
sheep

la cabra
goat

el cerdo
pig

la vaca
cow

24

el tractor
tractor

el riachuelo
stream

el puente
bridge

el campo
field

el bosque
forest

el heno
hay

la colina
hill

el espantapájaros
scarecrow

En la playa
On the Beach

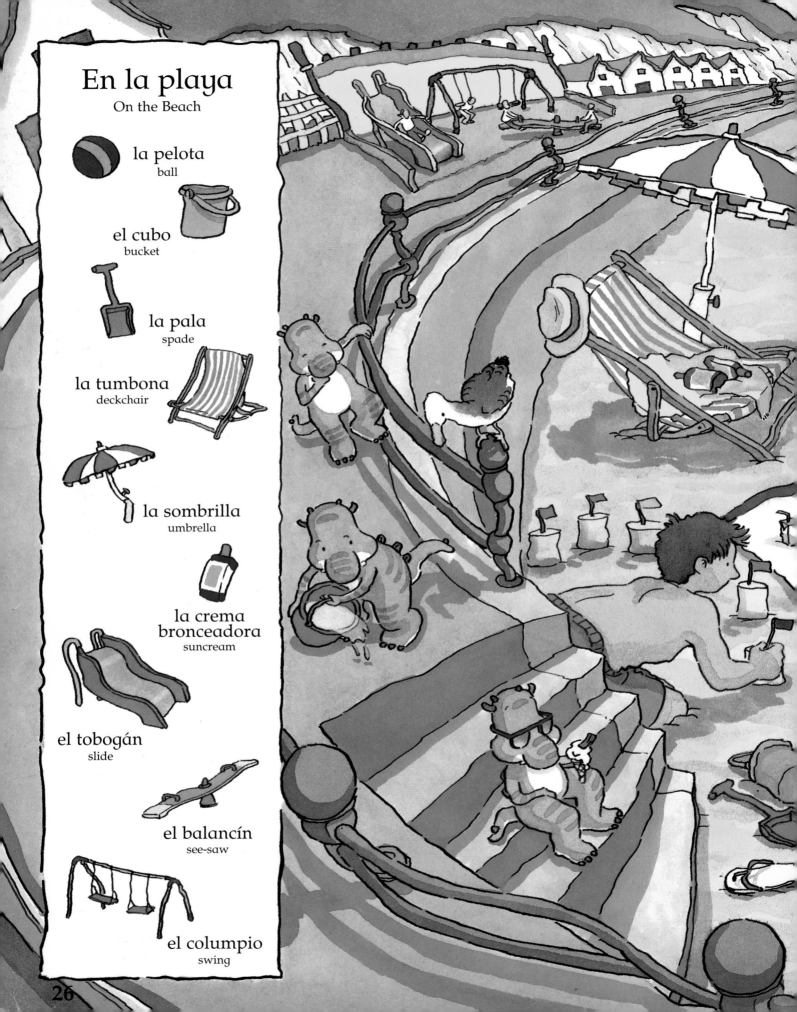

la pelota
ball

el cubo
bucket

la pala
spade

la tumbona
deckchair

la sombrilla
umbrella

la crema
bronceadora
suncream

el tobogán
slide

el balancín
see-saw

el columpio
swing

el barco
ship

el faro
lighthouse

el castillo de arena
sandcastle

la gaviota
seagull

la concha
shell

el cangrejo
crab

el pulpo
octopus

la estrella de mar
starfish

el alga
seaweed

27

La fiesta de cumpleaños

The Birthday Party

la tarjeta de cumpleaños
birthday card

la vela
candle

el globo
balloon

el regalo
present

la serpentina
streamer

el matasuegras
party blower

el gorro de papel
party hat

la varita mágica
wand

el mago
magician

28

los caramelos
sweets

el sándwich
sandwich

la pizza
pizza

el helado
ice cream

el chocolate
chocolate

la galleta
biscuit

la pajita
straw

la bebida
drink

el pastel
cake

Magia animal
Animal Magic

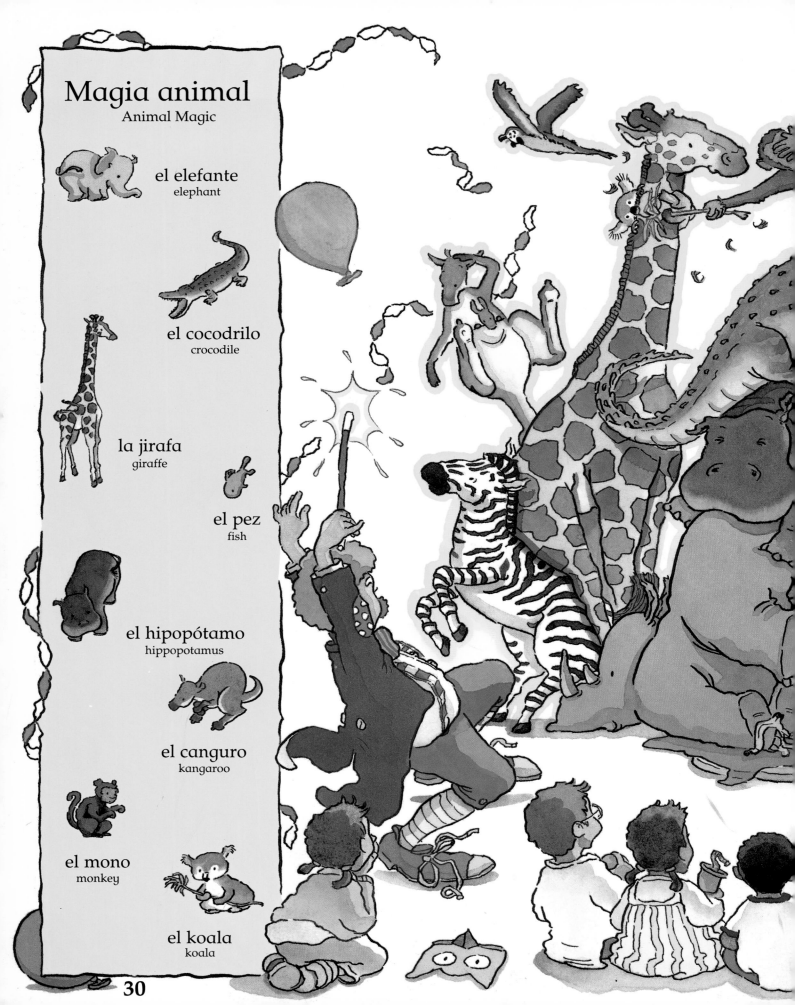

el elefante
elephant

el cocodrilo
crocodile

la jirafa
giraffe

el pez
fish

el hipopótamo
hippopotamus

el canguro
kangaroo

el mono
monkey

el koala
koala

el ratón
mouse

la morsa
walrus

el loro
parrot

el pingüino
penguin

el tigre
tiger

la cebra
zebra

el oso panda
panda

el rinoceronte
rhinoceros

La hora del baño
Bathtime

el vestido
dress

la cazadora
jacket

el jersey
jumper

los pantalones cortos
shorts

los calzoncillos
pants

la camisa
shirt

los zapatos
shoes

la falda
skirt

los calcetines
socks

los pantalones
trousers

la camiseta
T-shirt

el lavabo
basin

la bañera
bath

la toallita de
la cara
flannel

el espejo
mirror

la ducha
shower

el jabón
soap

la esponja
sponge

el váter
toilet

el papel
higiénico
toilet paper

el cepillo
de dientes
toothbrush

la pasta
de dientes
toothpaste

la toalla
towel

33

A la cama
In Bed

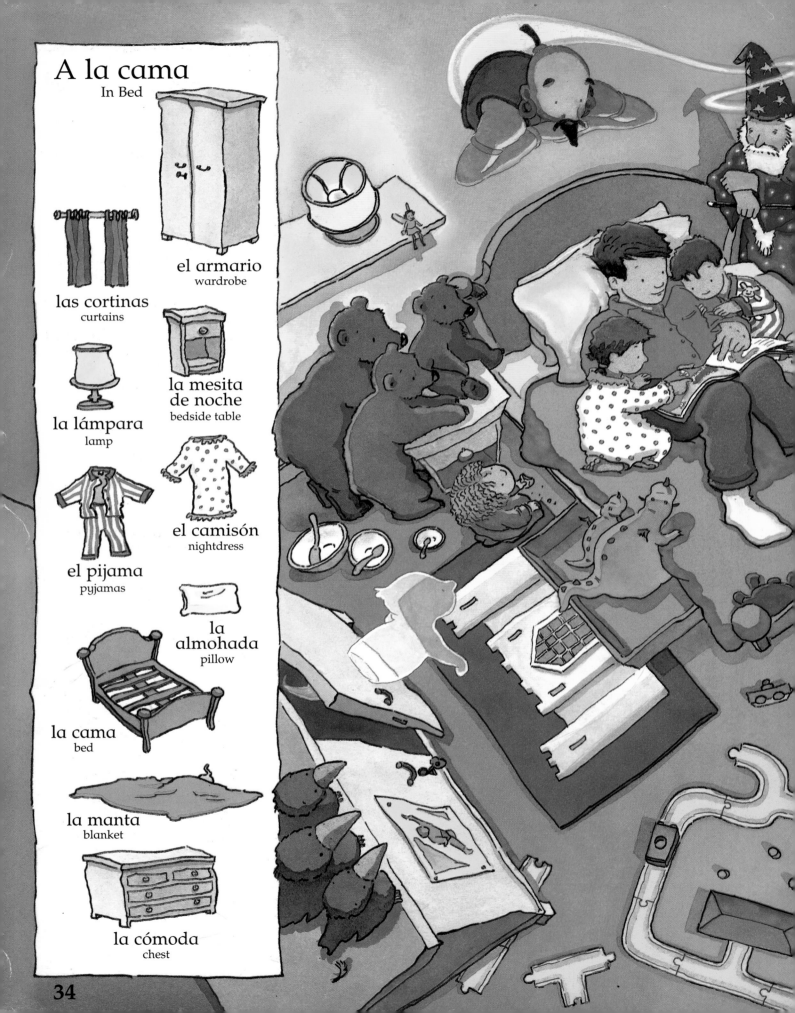

las cortinas
curtains

el armario
wardrobe

la lámpara
lamp

la mesita
de noche
bedside table

el pijama
pyjamas

el camisón
nightdress

la almohada
pillow

la cama
bed

la manta
blanket

la cómoda
chest

34

el cuento
storybook

el castillo
castle

el rey
king

la reina
queen

el genio
genie

la lámpara maravillosa
magic lamp

el dragón
dragon

el gigante
giant

Une cada palabra con su dibujo

Match the words with the pictures

el anillo
ring

la cabra
goat

los calcetines
socks

la campana
bell

la cebra
zebra

el clavo
nail

la furgoneta
van

el helicóptero
helicopter

la hormiga
ant

el huevo
egg

el malabarista
juggler

la marioneta
puppet

la mariquita
ladybird

la oruga
caterpillar

el paraguas
umbrella

el perro
dog

el pez
fish

el pulpo
octopus

el ratón
mouse

los rayos-X
x-ray

la reina
queen

el reloj
watch

el rey
king

el tigre
tiger

la tinta
ink

el yate
yacht

Vamos a contar

Lets Count

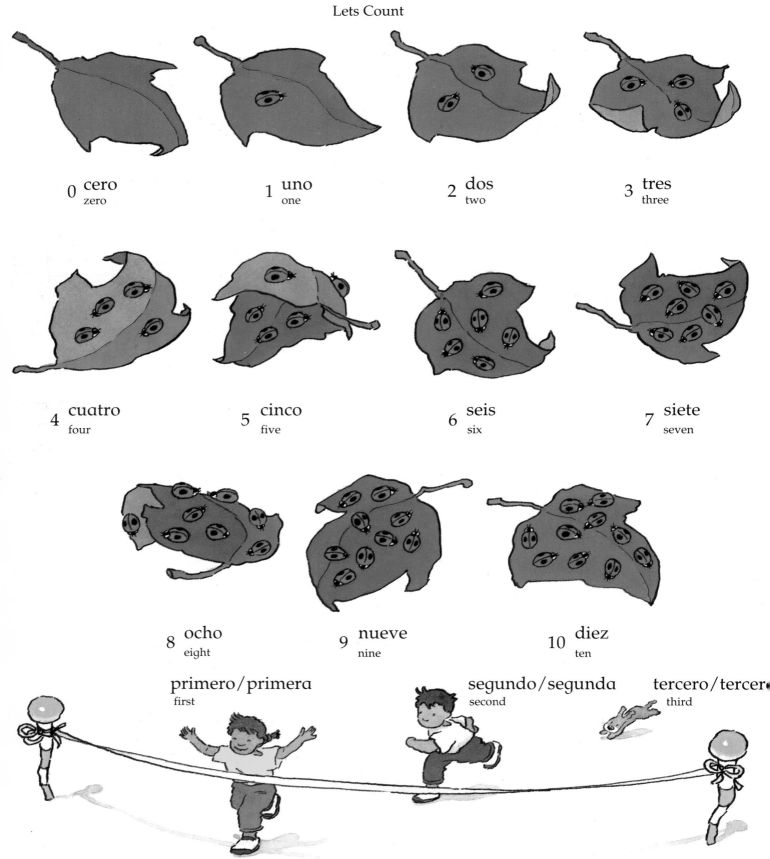

0 **cero**
zero

1 **uno**
one

2 **dos**
two

3 **tres**
three

4 **cuatro**
four

5 **cinco**
five

6 **seis**
six

7 **siete**
seven

8 **ocho**
eight

9 **nueve**
nine

10 **diez**
ten

primero/primera
first

segundo/segunda
second

tercero/tercer
third

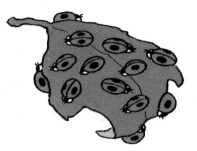

11 **once**
eleven

12 **doce**
twelve

13 **trece**
thirteen

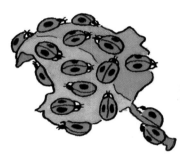

14 **catorce**
fourteen

15 **quince**
fifteen

16 **dieciséis**
sixteen

17 **diecisiete**
seventeen

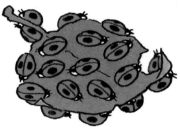

18 **dieciocho**
eighteen

19 **diecinueve**
nineteen

20 **veinte**
twenty

cuarto/cuarta
fourth

quinto/quinta
fifth

último/última
last

Formas
Shapes

el rectángulo
rectangle

el cuadrado
square

el círculo
circle

el corazón
heart

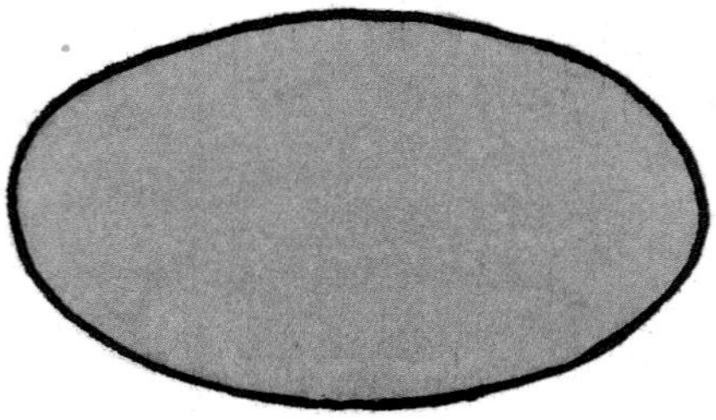

el óvalo
oval

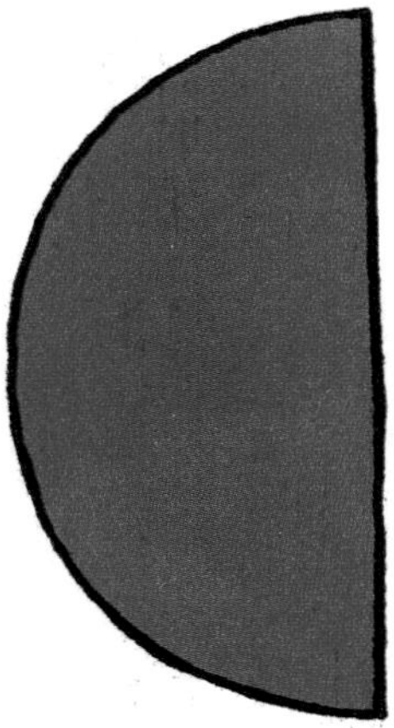

el semicírculo
semi-circle

la estrella
star

el triángulo
triangle

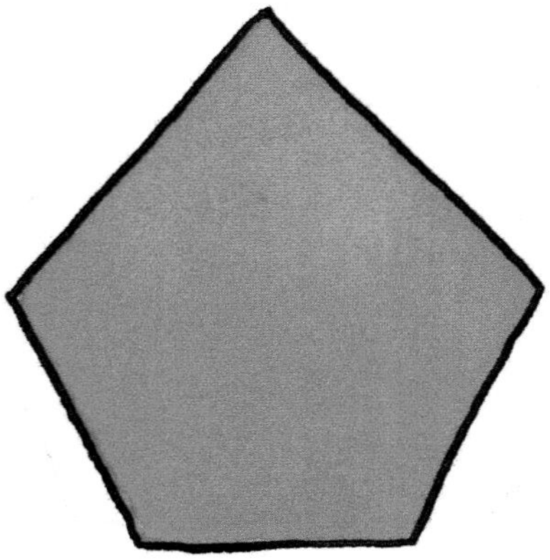

el pentágono
pentagon

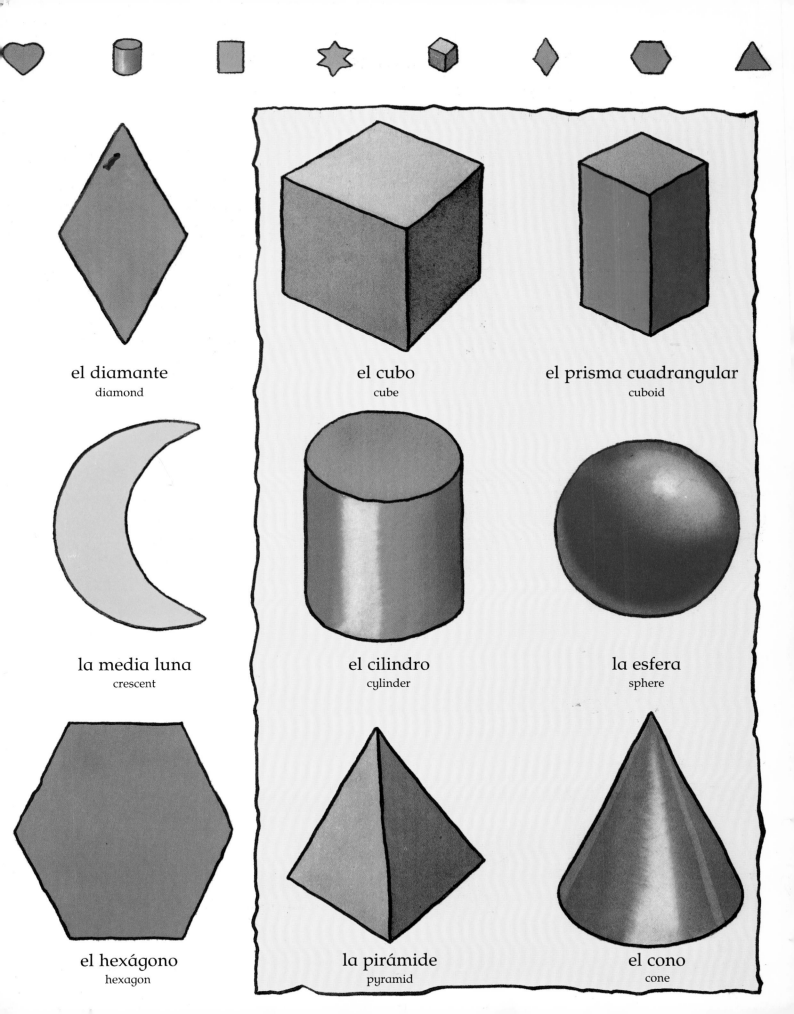

el diamante
diamond

la media luna
crescent

el hexágono
hexagon

el cubo
cube

el cilindro
cylinder

la pirámide
pyramid

el prisma cuadrangular
cuboid

la esfera
sphere

el cono
cone

Opuestos

Opposites

grande
big

pequeño/pequeña
small

limpio/limpia
clean

sucio/sucia
dirty

gordo/gorda
fat

delgado/delgada
thin

lleno/llena
full

vacío/vacía
empty

alto/alta
high

bajo/baja
low

caliente
hot

frío/fría
cold

nuevo/nueva
new

viejo/vieja
old

abierto/abierta
open

cerrado/cerrada
closed

oscuro/oscura
dark

iluminado/iluminada
light

rápido/rápida
fast

lento/lenta
slow

feliz
happy

triste
sad

pesado/pesada
heavy

ligero/ligera
light

largo/larga
long

corto/corta
short

más
more

menos
less

igual
same

diferente
different

mojado/mojada
wet

seco/seca
dry

43

El tiempo
The Weather

las nubes
cloudy

el sol
sunny

la lluvia
rainy

la nieve
snowy

el viento
windy

la niebla
foggy

La hora
The Time

las ocho en punto
eight o'clock

las diez en punto
ten o'clock

las doce del mediodía
twelve o'clock

las dos en punto
two o'clock

la cuatro en punto
four o'clock

las seis en punto
six o'clock

45

Index

46

playground	8
police officer	14
pop star	15
post bag	7
postman	14
potatoes	18
pottery	17
present	28
puppet	37
purple	12
pyjamas	34
pyramid (Egypt)	17
pyramid (shape)	41
Q queen	35, 37
R rabbit	7
racing car	22
rainy	44
recorder	23
rectangle	40
red	12
rhinoceros	31
ring	37
robot	22
roof	6
ruler	11
S sad	43
same	43
sandcastle	27
sandwich	29
saucepan	20
saucer	21
sausages	18
scarecrow	25
school	8
school bag	10
scissors	13
seagull	27
seaweed	27
second	38
see-saw	26
semi-circle	40
seven	38
seventeen	39
sheep	24
shell	27
ship	27
shirt	32
shoes	32
shop	8
short	43
shorts	32
shoulders	4
shower	33
six	38
sixteen	39
skeleton	16
skirt	32
slide	26
slow	43
small	42
snail	7
snowy	44
soap	33
socks	32, 37
sofa	21
soldier	17
spade	26
spaghetti	18
sphere	41
sphinx	17

spider	7
sponge	33
spoon	21
square	40
stairs	6
star	40
starfish	27
Stegosaurus	16
stereo	21
storybook	35
straw	29
stream	25
streamer	28
street	8
suncream	26
sunny	44
sweets	29
swing	26
T T-shirt	32
table	21
tambourine	23
teapot	21
teddy	22
teeth	5
television	21
ten	38
thin	42
third	38
thirteen	39
three	38
tiger	31, 37
time	45
toe	4
toilet	33
toilet paper	33
tomato	19
tongue	5
toothbrush	33
toothpaste	33
towel	33
tractor	25
traffic lights	8
train driver	15
train set	22
tree	7
triangle	40
Triceratops	16
trolley	18
trousers	32
truck	9
trumpet	23
tummy	4
twelve	39
twenty	39
two	38
Tyrannosaurus Rex	16
U umbrella	26, 37
V vacuum cleaner	21
van	37
vet	14
video recorder	21
W walrus	31
wand	28
wardrobe	34
washing machine	20
watch	37
wet	43
white	12
window	6
windy	44

X X-ray	37
Y yacht	37
yellow	12
yoghurt	19
Z zebra	31, 37
zebra crossing	8
zero	38

SPANISH:

A abierto/abierta	42
acera (f)	8
alga (f)	27
almohada (f)	34
alto/alta	42
amarillo (m)	12
ambulancia (f)	9
anillo (m)	37
araña (f)	7
árbol (m)	7
armario (m)	34
aspiradora (f)	21
astronauta (m)	15
autobús (m)	9
avión (m)	9
azul (m)	12
B bailarina (f)	15
bajo/baja	42
balancín (m)	26
bañera (f)	33
barbilla (f)	5
barco (m)	27
barriga (f)	4
bebida (f)	29
bicicleta (f)	9
blanco (m)	12
boca (f)	5
bol (m)	20
bollo (m)	18
bombero (m)	14
bosque (m)	25
brazo (m)	4
C caballete (m)	13
caballo (m)	24
cabeza (f)	4
cabra (f)	24, 36
cacerola (f)	20
caja registradora (f)	18
calcetines (m pl)	32, 37
caliente	42
calle (f)	8
calzoncillos (m pl)	32
cama (f)	34
camión (m)	9
camisa (f)	32
camiseta (f)	32
camisón (m)	34
campana (f)	36
campo (m)	25
cangrejo (m)	27
canguro (m)	30
cantante de pop (m)	15
cara (f)	5
caracol (m)	7
caramelos (m pl)	29
carpintero (m)	14
carro (m)	18
cartas (f pl)	7
cartera (f)	10
cartero (m)	14
cascabeles (m pl)	23

casete (m)	11
casita de muñecas (f)	22
castillo (m)	35
castillo de arena (m)	27
catorce	39
cazadora (f)	32
cebra (f)	31, 37
cepillo de dientes (m)	33
F cerámica (f)	17
cerdo (m)	24
cereales (m pl)	18
cero	38
cerrado/cerrada	42
cesta (f)	18
chimenea (f)	6
chocolate (m)	29
cilindro (m)	41
cinco	38
cinta de casete (f)	11
círculo (m)	40
coche (m)	9
coche de bomberos (m)	9
coche de carreras (m)	22
cocina (f)	20
cocinero (m)	15
cocodrilo (m)	30
codo (m)	4
cojín (m)	21
colegio (m)	8
colina (f)	25
columpio (m)	26
cómoda (f)	34
concha (f)	27
conductor de autobuses (m)	14
conductor de tren (m)	15
conejo (m)	7
cono (m)	41
corazón (m)	40
cortinas (f pl)	34
corto/corta	43
crema bronceadora (f)	26
cuadrado (m)	40
cuarto/cuarta	39
cuatro	38
cubo (m) (forma)	41
cubo (m) (para jugar)	26
cubo de la basura (m)	6
cuchara (f)	21
cuchillo (m)	20
cuello (m)	5
cuento (m)	35
cueva (f)	17
D dado (m)	11
dedo (m)	4
dedo gordo del pie (m)	4
delantal (m)	13
delgado/delgada	42
diamante (m)	41
dibujo (m)	13
diecinueve	39
dieciocho	39
dieciséis	39
diecisiete	39
dientes (m pl)	5
diez	38
diferente	43
Diplodocus (m)	16
disquete (m)	11
doce	39

47